S0-EQD-217

NORTH POMFRET POEMS

NORTH POMFRET

POEMS

SONGS OF LIFE, LOVE, AND DEATH

FOR FOUR SEASONS

1968 – 1993

Peter Fox Smith

PETER FOX SMITH

ACKNOWLEDGMENTS

Through the efforts and the expertise of three friends this book came to be. Barbara Saine laboriously, and with ever-present cordiality, typed the manuscript. Robert Grinnell, whose continuing enthusiasm for all my work is a great encouragement, read the manuscript and offered perceptive suggestions. Finally, Glenn Suokko, with his considerable knowledge, his good taste, and an uncanny ability to discern immediately my desires, made of that manuscript this beautiful book.

© 1995 Peter Fox Smith
Library of Congress Catalog Number 95-92725
ISBN 0-9649612-0-2

CONTENTS

Dedication ix
Prologue xi

PART ONE: WINTER
    North Pomfret Hills 3
    Matter Resolves Not Into Spirit 3
    One A:M December Fifth, 1791 5
    December Night 6
    California Corpulent Christmas Cantata 8
    An American Yule Anthology: 1973 9
    A Korean War Poem 11
    The Man Who With His Python Slept 12
    Reverence 13
    First Prayer 15
    False Spring 15
    February Moon 16
    The Franklin Stove 19
    February Thaw 21
    Jesus The Star Conqueror 22
    Three Excerpts From "A Vermont Road Journal" 24
    Oh, She Loves Winter's Hushed Beauty 26
    Ever Through The Subways Of Our Lives 27
    How Else Other Than It Is 28
    So It's March Again 28
    ski boy ski 29
    Willow Tree In Winter 31
    In Just One Poem Could You Not Flap Your Cynic Wings? 32
    This Morning You Stood In The March Sun 35
    Roving 36
    By Barn Door Waits 37

PART TWO: SPRING
    Temptress Spring Stirred Blazing Thoughts 40
    Two Refrains 41
    Eat 41
    Two Lines of Discontent 42

Spring Storm Requiem	42
Ars Poetica Again	43
Pilgrim Comes Home	44
The A, B, C's Of Cyril's Holiday	45
Daddy Disconsolate	47
Splitting Wood In Spring	48
Deductions Of A College Freshman	49
Burial Of The Blond Girl's Cat	50
Mensuration 1,2,3 Or Something About Sady	52
Excerpt From "The Good Friday Spell" Of Wagner's *Parsifal*	53
May	55
The Figment	56
First Vignette From A Nearby Village	56
Second Vignette From A Nearby Village	58
Senta For The Dutchman Sang	59
Image	59
I Visit Bob	60
The Brook	63
Some Spirit Minus Matter	64

PART THREE: SUMMER

Rummage Sale	66
Rilke's "Archaic Torso Of Apollo"	68
Six Meditations From A Sheepdog's Reveries	69
The Youths	72
Poseidon With His Trident	72
Tetrad	75
The Water In The Holy Stream	76
West Coast Of Ireland	76
The Odd Job Neighbor	77
Green Growing Fierce In Force	78
Witness The Words Of One Without	79
On Looking For Carolyn	80
Song Of Farewell	82
Mordicai "Pistachio" Mumford's Poetry Sampler	82
"He Who Once The Barnyard Ruled"	83

Ballad Of Hannah The Hitchhiker	84
A Medieval Romance	85
A Modern Romance	86
Two Excerpts From "The Isagogics Of Joshua Winters"	87
Gaudeamus	88
An Ode For Our Time	89
Two Fragments From Summertime	89
Burial Ground	90
Perhaps Spirit Can Exceed Matter	91

PART FOUR: FALL

How Fast Fall Falls	98
To Christmas Cove	99
Two Songs	102
Indian Summer	103
Ars Apologia In Sonata Form	103
I'll Climb To Old Red's Grave	105
On Making Love	106
Arthur King's Hills	109
Around The Robin Egg, Aroo	111
Ternion	111
Bare Rump To Rump Old Lovers Lie	112
I Am A Red Sox Fan	113
October Rains	113
Proem And Poem	115
Three Vagrants	116
Two Sonnets Of A Sort As One Something	116
Dromedary Dogmatik	117
Is The Vermont Visitor Viennese?	118
Late Fall Night Before Slaughter	119
When Men Created Gods	120
On The Manner By Which Matter Becomes Spirit	121
Threnodies	123
Epilogue	126

About the Author	128

To Joanne

THERE ARE NO TIMES

There are no times when in this crazy, mixed-
Up head but happy heart I do not know
How love, our vast affection, firmly fixed
In the circumference of our needs, and fixed,
Somehow, in remnants of our youth which goes
Far back beyond the marriage bed to basics
Of the mortal span, does not keep us through blows
Of tree uprooting winds. So much I know.

And little else, if any else, of this
Terraqueous clash, inane and quick, with
Cruel, prompt time do perceive, nor else need
To glean, or no more ask of wide, mute
Spheres yet, regular as monks at prayers, I plead
Fierce fates allow us to expire our deed.

" A poem is a composition written for performance by the human voice."
– Jon Stallworthy

PROLOGUE

"As is the generation of leaves, so is that of humanity.
The wind scatters the leaves on the ground, but the live timber
burgeons with leaves again in the season of spring returning.
So one generation will grow while another dies."

– Book VI, Lines 145–151 of *The Iliad* by Homer

That single leaf,
Maple, Beech, or
Birch, perhaps, so
Often likened
Unto our lives,
Poet's symbol
Of passing time,
From age to age,
Generations
Seemlessly one
In the next to
Endless cycles
Moving, turning,
Fleeting, gone-by,
Buds bursting in
These beautiful
Hermit hills of
North accustomed
Trees brief growing,
Short, terse, urgent
Seminations
Which teem about
Us only to
Disappear in
Fast swirling snows
Months and months of
Flake piling on
Flake in mountain
Mass unmeasured

Long frozenness
Of one season
Some say who think
Ever we live
In winter's fold
Long arms holding
The many months
Which is what the
Tourist is told:

"How long is your
  Winter here?" asked
  The tourist at
  The village store.

"Eleven months
  Of winter, one
  Of late fall," the
  Farmer replied.

The seasons pass
So fast the days
We cannot count
From bud to red
Wrinkled leaves or
Brown blown away
In chill winds of
Autumn remnants
Spreading aged
Determinents
Helter-skelter
Wings spanning wide
Pastures, valleys
To sky high hills
Unrepenting;
Unrelenting!
We lift up our
Eyes and see cold
Dominating.

Cold dominant;
Sub-dominant
Snow and frozen
Aspects pervade
Each dimension
Of north domain
How well we know
Yet each autumn
Severely new
Respect resounds
Across a field
Quickly frozen
Hard as a stone
Along its spine
A leaf blowing
Swirls, ceases, and

Moves ever on
Prancing, dancing
Through white gauzy
Vacillations
Behold the snow.
We wait. Spring sings
A laughing song,
Our gardens swell
With flower, food,
And fragrances
Everlasting
From fall to fall
Even though our songs,
Our loves, our needs,
Oh, so quickly
Pass leaf to leaf.

WINTER

NORTH POMFRET HILLS

Water-color grey and white,
Surely, blown by the winds of my coming,
The clouds move north,
Patterned
For long fingers of light to reach through,
To pet the yielding hills,
All feminine,
Buttocks and breasts of the land,
Round rising,
Softly
Frocked in the brown and grey
Of a snowless December day.

What will the hills be
When my dying is done?
Who will take the restless wind
For loving?

MATTER RESOLVES NOT INTO SPIRIT

I

Solitude and alone
Are not the same.
Quiet, in these hills,
Lies like sun upon the pond.
Gaze into space beyond
The dimmest star:
Space, time, matter;
That's all there is.
No spirit there. In your
Dearest words, your most
Intimate touch, be assured,

You only have yourself!
Oh, you can believe in other things

As long as you remember
Matter resolves not into spirit.
A moon is but a moon
And an accident this earth
Without a purpose or a plan,
A senseless part of the very vast
Where all drifts toward
Darkness, cold, and dust.
And remember, no one has
Ever found a human soul.

II

Yet there may be some love
Comingling blood and bone
As bodies swell with song.
Finite is the hour, indeed,
That to deny is to deceive,
Yet there may be love,
Some irrepressible urge
To reach beyond our reach
And to affirm.

III

The seas shine,
Mountains climb within the clouds,
And far fields lie flat
Until the earth bends round.
Whatever the doubt or pain
For a few hours
Something says assert
And we respond:
Some with a reaching out,
Some locked so into a self
They cannot see beyond.

IV

Alone in all this we are

But it matters how we look
Upon that dimmest star:
For some with a love spanning out;
For others, one that rots within.

One a:m December Fifth, 1791

(The Death of Mozart)

In that early
Morning darkness
Of a candle's
Flicker glowing,
Another light
Expired. Silver
In its gleaming,
Or gold, or a

"Light of sunbeams"*
We can't define
(Its color is
Not the issue).
Out! Gone! And yet,
More than when those
Premonitions
Of an end near,

And many debts,
And sickness of
Fevered brain cost
Yielding those last
Notes which we will
Never know, a

Luminance spreads
Across our sphere;
Shimmering strings,
Trilling winds, and

*The Irish tenor Michael Kelly, who first sang the roles of Basilio and Curzio, said that when Mozart was excited his eyes were bright and his appearance so animated that it would be "as impossible to describe it, as it would be to paint sunbeams."

Choral voices
Conjoining in
"Ave verum"
Ensembles which

Transform distress
Into glowing,
Earthly sheening
By that light snuffed
In a pauper's
Grave still shinning,

Still singing its
Radiant song.

December Night

I

The twisted fingers of my tallest beech,
It is really me that does the belonging,
Lie still across the moon's holy white
Grey-boned check

And like argent bracelets on gypsy arms
And rings on every finger
The haughty Hemlock branches show
Their snow.

The brook rings in its silver shoes
And the black jawbone sky arches
Sleeping wings around the turn
Of our hills

And while I walked, the sheepdog
And I, the no man's land stars
Flickered and beat against my jumping
Stomach's wall.

Thirty years dissolved this night;
A boy again received the virgin
World unmediated in his mindless
Humming heart.

    II

My God! One could almost
Believe in god again; almost
Forget what happens when
The sun pulls

Its red eye up onto the ice blue
Morning sky and the children
Arise to rattle and
To jar the

Very teeth in the great mother's
Holy face. One, on such a
December night, could almost
Believe in

God again if his heart could
Overrun the head and he could
Forever forget that he is one
Of much too many men.

He could almost believe
In god once more
Were it not for too many people,
Most of whom are poor.

California Corpulent Christmas Cantata

Does any
One know
If many
Are fat in
San Luis
O bis
Po?

Ho!
Ho, Ho, Ho!

Santa comes
To quaint
Morro Bay
And
San Luis
O bis
Po

And
He is fat.

But I don't know
If he's
The only
Jolly one
That's fat
In
San Luis
O bis
Po.

Ho!
Ho! Ho! Ho!

An American Yule Anthology: 1973

I
(Christmas)

Viennese crescents baking
At Christmas time drag
Recollections up from
Psychic graves buried
In boyhood like Christ
In an Easter tomb for
Annual resuscitation on
A birthday, or so say
Matthew, Mark, and Luke
(Not even pen names these
Mere pseudonyms of redactors)

And thus I think of a white Church
Of New England simplicity, on
My old street, before the building fund
Renovated square-head hand made nails,
Where the ". . . and it came to pass
There went out a decree . . ." was read this time
Each year by a minister who
Spoke his "Dearly Beloved" way into the
Pockets of middle-class parishioners,
Razed the little church, in its
Stead built a monument to money,

And continued the killing of Jesus the Christ.
Powdered-sugared crescents melting in mouths
Of brothers home from Sunday School,
An afternoon waiting for their whims.
They are fathers now, without a
Christ, with sons of counting eyes
Watching crescents baking through the
Window of the oven door, more anxious
Than the third day ascent of a bent,
Sore, broken, stapled Jew, one spring morn,
Born they say, they who never were,

WINTER

Thirty-three years before
On Christmas day for
Unto you this day
In the city of it makes
A nice story
Or does it really
Shit on straw under star
Frankincense and myrrh
But no crescents.
There is a lot more Christmas left
In cookies than in Christ.

    II
(New Year)

Bury the year seventy-three
In graves dug with wine
Courageously

Fondling in midnight grope
The small bra equipped breast
Of Hope,

Your neighbor's shy, mousy wife
You've often seen across the lawn of
Middle-life

While Auld Lang Syne is
Spread thin again by old Guy
And his

Royal Canadian music men to flat
Champagne as desperate cheer under
Silly hats

Exudes while no one pays
For a better booze to toast
The Day.

Ah, that we are but
Shadows on a wall,
Deep within the fire lit
Cave, no exit on the wall,

Slave to electro-chemical
Energy tugging on our
Sleeve with no Buddha
Or no Socrates

To show the way
There is no way
To show a way
To go O so

Late now, gone Guy's
Once a year music men
Iceless diluted whiskey in
One hand clutching

The other free for
Hope's recycled breast
Passed guest to guest
You feel it sleeping

Now before the dawn
Of hang-over rest
Where Bloody Marys will
Arouse football on TV.

A Korean War Poem

(January 27, 1973)

Let us praise the peace
And the peace-makers,
Noble men bandying one
War for another.

Sound the guns, gorilla guns
The scratching pen inks the end.
Sound the guns, gorilla guns
And watch a celebrating soldier bend

Toward death. Cease fire!
The order read but he is dead.
Who will tell his mother why?
Parade horns,

And victory songs,
Hat tossing hoots and howls.
You can see it's over.
The Peace it has been signed!

Sound the guns, gorilla guns
Dance drunk in khaki socks.
Sound the guns, gorilla guns
He was sent home in a box

Gift-wrapped in Old Glory.

The Man Who With His Python Slept

The man who with his Python slept,
Lovingly, for eight grateful years,
Three legs entwined as one, wept,
Cried, and sobbed the day his serpent
Died. Now, at sixty-six, his light
Each night suggests he is awake
Much now that he is alone. Quite
A shock it was, I guess, for him
To lose his love. I recall how
They would play in their study. Trim,
Indeed, he was in shape for a
Gent his age for they would wrestle
By the hour, then curl in repose.
I suppose he may never love again.

Reverence

(Or the verb to subtract utilized in a Florida winter Holiday)

"Reverence: the spiritual attitude of a man to a god and a dog to a man."
                                – Ambrose Bierce

    I

How pleasant to press bare-foot prints
into white sand of Florida beach anon
flushed away to sea just as each day,

because the steps are days of a career,
some of us slowly is subtracted for
there is no sin of omission here.

After addition we learned subtraction
(is it the same with the new math?),
multiplication, division, and fractions.

    "Look at this olive shell—
      Perfect for our collection."
    "Give it back to God."
    "But you don't believe in God."
    "Give it back to it anyway."

Bring our feet together from far scatterings
of private play in waves, in books, in
hooking fish, in muse of sun. Bring us all

together, small car, for tenure like
tires turn and turn us into telamon
or tidbits for hungry Tellus. Goodbye.

    "That'll be five-eighty with tax
     an I than kya, Sa, an yall cum
     back ta see us agin, ya hea."

>   ("And you all, Sir, contain a
>   surplus of politeness. Yanks talk
>   tourist with undivided tongue.")

II

From the green hills of the little towns
where cows, variegated black and white,
are grazing, monosyllabic, that is quite terse,

But bright and measured straight, a
dialog with Vermont's bus driver strikes
silence across a New Yorker's touring face.

"You can't get on the bus, Mista, witha dog."
"Who said I can't get on the bus with my dog?"
"The rule says you can't get on witha dog."
"Well, you can take your goddamn bus and stuff
 it you know where."
"And you can board the god
 damn bus if you do likewise with your dog."

III

Notice now, in the juxtaposition of dog and god,
something curious. Neither malaprop nor
palindrome, one is simply the other, backwards.

Canine Creator? Immortal mut?
Did someone feed the dog? O my God,
do not ever forget to feed the Dog!

There is no mathematics in this.
It is but a matter of being on the safe side.
Remember old Pascal's wager?

>   "We'll return. We'll come
>   back to visit for mothers
>   and fathers migrate here

WINTER

to die.
 Elementary subtraction; it is
 called, 'giving it back to God.'"

First Prayer

(From "Seven Prayers to an Empty Sky")

Thoughts splattered, nerves torn,
We look outside ourselves for succor of mere
Morsels to drop from an empty sky whose reach
So far out-strips the mortal eye
That a poor pittance of a self
Shrinks, implodes to nothing,
And conjures up some human
Love and aged alcohol, something for
Both hands, to subdue us
Each day before we grapple with the next.

How the palaestra swarms like balls
Of newborn snakes with human fray
While the sun, like honey on hot bread,
Rolls towards a far corner.

False Spring

When here in late January I stand
Black-booted in horse-shit and hay,
Potpourri of barnyard tidying, rake and
Shovel hand to hand, and hear the

Brook bel cantoing April airs after
A night of vernal rain, hoof-high
Mares flicking past toward the
Pasture where, like a tired whore,

Reclines a bale of last summer's hay, and,
Finding no south warm bird, no sprouts
Of green reaching through receding snow,
I know it is in me a false spring which

Stirs up garden days and company of trout
In ponds of summer afternoons under
Tumescent clouds, I know the punch of hard
Winter still will reel me to deal with

Frozen pipes, dead cars, and a family crouched
Before the stove forestalling sleep between
Long, wide icy sheets.

FEBRUARY MOON

(In Memory of my Mother: Alice Johnson Smith)

    Prologue

The round moon sliding on the February sky
urged words from me, or through me, as the pagan
poet would say, for here they lie,
stuck upon the page, locked into the eye.

Do you expect sweet descriptions in worn verse,
beams painting paths down the aisle of night,
(I'm tempted to try another that's even worse,
the kind that rhymers use to fill their purse

with royalties from the home-folk magazines)
or the nonsense, as some call it, of modern poetry
where, formless and rhymeless, to many it seems,
meaningless words evoke neither hopes nor dreams,

nor stir in us those thoughts of human worth.
Back to the February moon. Translated into words
what does it say about a reason for birth
into some snow stalled farm pinned to earth

by four who have made it a home? The odds improve.
They may see the cycling seasons circle into years.
They may yet record one generation move
to another as the ancient way follows the groove

of touchless time, gone but back and always here
and always running on. Or what does that
bouncing sun's light, for that is what we are
told the moon's light is, reveal from spaces far

about death, that certain cold, still end of space
and time put away forever in a box or maintained
as ashes in an urn? Can we better face
such facts having stood beneath a thin trace

of the February moon, arching brain and brow
to the cold white light? Perhaps the
translation makes some difference. I maintain
the examples which follow will explain:

    1.

Born to the February moon
on some farm's winter night,
the winds interminable tune
sang of their joy and fright.

She grew strong and straight,
her long black hair marking
the barefooted dancing gait
of her long summer larking.

The omens had seemed so good,
a gift from winter's moon.
But no great sage stood
ready to read the rune

of her long sacking illness
and her death one June.

2.

Daughter of Aquarius
round full moon
O sött Natt*
A lonely call from a northland loon
You miss her swimming in your
fish-filled waters.

No girl lived her youth so much alone
to hunt the duck
to land the dinner bass.
Hear the lonesome call from a northland loon.
She left her husband and two sons

to die in June.

3.

Fish eyes
lift to see the waters crease
long white limbs descending
brunette hairs arching over
the waters broken edge

alone
caught in nature's rhyme,
practitioner of bird and snake,
shell and fish, Poseidon's girl,
parting the water

Pain born life
O sweet night
Aquarian moon
fish fated

swimming she
watersnake
duck bass
shell stone sand

*Oh sweet night
(Swedish)

18

WINTER

god lived
she lived
he died
she's dead

in June.

      E p i l o g u e

The February moon speaks nothing.
Like any other moon we beneath impose
on it our fragile human mood;
the ecstasies of lovers
or that which the tortured brood.

THE FRANKLIN STOVE

   (An undramatic monologue)

It has been two years, or maybe three,
since I wrote about the Franklin stove
in our Vermont living room ($75.00
third-hand and so this year we drove

three days to find two more to heat the
second floor and third). What I wrote
then, proceeding now from memory, was
fancy with a cosmic turn. A quotation

would let you see what I mean but I
doubt if it is important. You'll take my
word. What could I say if I bring the
subject down to earth? I wonder why

it seems easier to speak in symbols
of the flames than to speak of flames
themselves as if they weren't important
for exactly what they are, warm flames

in our stove. I'll not reduce them to
philosophy this deep February night
(the moon it passed with my last poem)
in the concocted words I need to write

to keep my rhymes. She lies in sleep
before the wilting flames yet
knows the fire is there and then,
when ashes lie barely red, she'll get

up and hike the narrow stairs to where
we sleep to join me in bed. The stove

looks not the same by day as night.
Morning's imperfections, a lost piece,
a patch of rust, a block under leg to
keep it level on the hearth, decrease

its value only if you collect for the
auction block for they are never seen
at night when quick flames and the lamp
of kerosene produce a gentle mean

of light between too bright and no light
at all (when I stumble on the stairs
or bang in the hall on way to see what
has, at 3 A.M., the dog bark till it wears

upon my sleep and hers). We started
to fix it up. The missing piece is but
a small ring, we'll find that, the rust
we rub a way with steel wool, but

the little block under the leg will
stay. A little imperfection tells a
discerning eye the way New Englanders
make life go right in frozen hills today

as in those early days when life was really
hard, before we played at living like our
ancestors whose stoves in no way gave just
pretty light but kept them hour by hour.

February Thaw

February thaw
in sudden turn to
cold sealed our culvert
thick in ice redeemed

swing by swing
chip by chip
swing by swing
drip by drip

from splitting wedge
at handled edge
of aching triceps
against the moratory

mother of us all
(immortal and tough)

she cannot seduce
me to tropical grants
free fund avocado
or orange on every tree

to forget these bouts with her

ice frost flood drought
"I'll get you after all"
all of which I know but
as yet owns not all of me.

Jesus the Star Conqueror

I
("An then shall they see the Son of man coming in the clouds with great power and glory."
— Mark, 13.26)

Jesus the star conqueror;
Vanquisher of demons.
Can he be conquered?

Is it time for time
To play its game
With the human heart
Making Jesus to depart
As ancient star and myth
Once fled?

Does time have a new
Game to play?
Jesus to degrate?

Were he to come again,
Said Kafka,
It would be too late!

II
("One shall not live by bread alone")

Once there was a dainty fate,
Couched in Christian hope,
But now it is belligerent
And cleans like Lava Soap

The hidden facts and horrible lies
In Cardinal Charlie's vague replies
To wonderings if heaven's real
Or whether bread and wine make a meal.

One can't live on bread alone
And wine is costly much
So hungry people hobble and roam
For such is such and such

Is such and such is such
Is such.

      III
("The Last Supper")

In the moment of doing
We undo.
Vague is the noontime news
Broadcast for coffers and
Resonant voiced fun.
In the moment of undoing
It is done.

Cabs are hard to find
And free rides are few.
We do in the undoing
What we repair
With glue:

Drink this glue,
Break this lead
This is my Last Supper
Before I take to bed.

This is my Last Supper
Before I lie in bed,
Fastened by secreted glue,
Anchored by digested lead.

Three Excerpts from a "Vermont Road Journal"

After Weeks Words Again

Nursed,
mid-winter snow,
like skin of middle
age,

stretched
taut, lies less white,
more used. "Did I
hear middle age?"

carp the crows, arrow-beaked,
floating tails, wings reaching
black,
"Did I hear middle age?"

Oh,
so ebony sheen,
Barnard-Bethel-Black,
progression through
three:

    White snow
    Grey hill
    Black crow.

White
reaching black;
progressions cease!

Driving past
the flexing waters running down
their rocks,

nerves,
knawed by a thousand rats,
neared their end.

Mountain Pass

Ice
of winter way,
arming mountain
rock,

like
medieval knight,
aegis silver

sheen,
freeze all thought
of is and ought

and let us feel love's
unfettered dream.

Ice Storm

It was his last morning
before the mirror.
Combusting from the pretty sight,
O Narcissus in us all,

he did not know,
while
he drew the Schick
through

lime scented cream,
how
the roads
were slick.

OH, SHE LOVES WINTER'S HUSHED BEAUTY

Oh,
She loves winter's
Hushed beauty but
Not so much of it

And intones laments
Of no garden greens
Or purple blooms or blue

While
Quietly he chants
Solemn praises of
A world renewed below
Three feet of virgin snow;
Of the wild blizzard's blow,

Of white skies,
Of no flies,

And winds of ice
Clean upon his face
As old snowshoes
Mark him to a
Private pagan place

Of sainted pines;
A deep sanctuary
With rocky shrines
Where storms of solitude
Cleanse and denude

Time much fribbled by

Public plots,
Social schemes,

And other forced means
Of a diminished rectitude.

Ever through the Subways of Our Lives

(Boston)

Ever
Through the subways of our
Lives
Terrestrial travel ends
In
Genitals, a token for the
Trip,
Commuter jostled among screech-squeal
Of
Metal wheel, jostled under hard lights

Where journals bearing news of
Hate,
Suffering, theft, and deaths
Are
Read while *"Winter ist vergangen
Nicht"**
Nor jonquils rise through April melting
Snow
In innocence, standing like youths untold

Of
Backache and bedlam but
One
Stop away — "End of the line!"
"'Board,"
Barely I hear through the boscage
Of
Human clutter everywhere. Glad be
That
Boccherini is ringing in my ear.

*"Winter is not gone" is a line from a German song.

How Else Other Than It Is

How else, other than it is, could the world be:
Steeped in grief, joys fleet blaze, and the
Appointed end, dumb and sad but welcome?
How else could it be?

And should you answer Yes, otherwise,
Ponder well and long for cosmic bonds
Do not cut easily. Without hate what is our
Love? And we must eat.

Whatever is, is right, here in this the best
Of all possible worlds? I did not say that.
Rather, whatever is, is the way it is,
Because, how else,

For we are what we are, how else
Could it be? What else could we do or be
Within the punctual steps of commissioned
Time, or a space confined

To some esoteric relativity? And so let us
Rise to each days light to touch with
Art-filled hands our craft, to live and to love
As well as we can.

So It's March Again

So it's March again and spring seems early this year
The roads already ruts of April mud as snows disappear

We think of seeds of getting gardens plowed
But that's two months away and we'll be endowed

By hard-surrendering winter storms before May
Is it the six long months of snow and slow decay

Of my bones which has me think this way
Or just unconscious fret over finances or hay

Enough for horses I lie in bed elbow propped to write
Listening to your piano-forte diffuse airs throughout the night

And wonder what will spring bring to our farm
What after spring what of fall of winter next my arm

Has work to do yet lies quiet in its sleeve months pass

In reverie as I day-dream of what would be
Were I to work one desire to actuality

Food for cold days of snow and wood piled
High for blizzard blows but I am not reconciled

To routine my damn books intervene ideas materialize
Inviting me to their lair to cerebrate what and why
And I let brown earth go bare I let your eyes

Wonder about the farm and I attired in isolation
Wonder about our silly spin pawled for one direction
And the doleful destination

Of my March musings.

ski boy ski

(For Peter: Winter 1971)

i

ski boy ski
ski cock-legged
over her crystal chin
along her shadowed nape of neck
down her frozen breast

fish fire fast
ski boy ski

before the quaking hours
slither into dusk their hungry to the
bone fingers folding over your unprecedented
play removing you from
a long arms length
to empty lands
so very far away
ski boy ski

ii

"One must be responsible"
(ski boy ski)
"Have you done your homework?"
(ski boy ski)
"Practice your music"
(ski boy ski)
"Work before play"
(ski boy ski)

iii

ski boy ski
ski your whipping heart
over her stomach soft and round
blessed smooth and round
wedel down her long thin thigh
her long thin thigh
wedel through her bewitching eye
ski boy ski

ski
whistling thoughts wind running
your honey gold legs
untroubled
ski the circling sun
from edge to edge

ski the dream dark dreams
to dreamless sleep
ski her sinless virgin skin
ski boy ski

i v

ski boy ski
ski until the hill is gone
ski its chalice
ski its grail
ski until you stand alone
tired legs
skis in hand
at the edge of the recalcitrant edge
of an endless land's unresolved new trail
ski boy ski

and
ski
ski boy ski
smiles into the sweet wind
and kiss the wind
kiss her long for me
and wend your lickty-split
heart and head
home again
but
ski boy ski

WILLOW TREE IN WINTER

I

So small, four or
Six swirled and frayed
Brown, dead leaves of
   Willow tree's

Limp, long branches
Down doddering
In rimy winds.
   Wondering,

Displaced, I bide
Harsh moils of need
Jounced like twigs of
   Willow tree.

II

Snow swallowing
Minutes over
Those lean leaves spin
   Unretrieved,

Far dispersed yet
Burrowing what
Remains of me,
   Pondering

Terrible dreams,
Assuaged, it seems,
By a moody
   Willow tree.

IN JUST ONE POEM COULD YOU NOT FLAP YOUR CYNIC WINGS?

I

"In just one poem could you not flap your cynic wings
With mocking undulations of fancy flight
To note some good in things?

Can you not derive from past great deeds
In words which please

The very seeds
Through which we can grow anew?"

    II

"Gardens sprout toxic weeds,
  Rusty waters reek,
  There is more garbage than there is ground,
  And poisoned air makes black and sick our lungs
  While politicians climb
  The wrungs
  Of power
  Abandoning us
  To speculate
  A dire fate!"

    III

"That is precisely what I mean!
  Your words never mend.
  They only tear apart.
  Negative and nasty
  They offend the head,
  Malign the heart,
  And do not inspire."

    IV

"Not all poems dote on goodness, truth, or beauty.
  Crass or crude some lead
  Some to a different duty.
  No polished or lofty words expect from me.
  I spread my verbal wings
  To fly and dive into the vortex of decay.
  I will not perch and pose and with pretty words
  Simply hope our ills away!

  What we need to do,
  Not just your way nor mine,
  But together,

And not because I love you because I don't,
But because it involves each of us,
Is to fix the problem which we must fix."

    V

"And precisely what is that problem which we must fix?"

    VI

"People!
  Too goddamn many people everywhere.
We must sterilize.
Neuter!
We must control both the parts
Which incessantly mindlessly mix
With every urge!
Most of the problems
Which you can name —
From poverty to pollution and
From the homeless to hunger —
We can blame

On too many people!

We cannot clothe or feed
All those we have got
But we go on making more and more and more
Without limits.

And we hurt
And we hunger;
We hate
And we make war!

Should I suppose
That only when we have killed our neighbor,
Knawed his bones,
Usurped his home,
And raped his daughter and his wife that then

We can sit in his chair contentedly and exclaim
'This is the life?'"

VII

Somewhere pure breezes wave grassy plains,
Somewhere waves break on unsullied shores,
And somewhere still in the white of full-moon
Nights natives chant their ancient, sacred lore.

Somewhere still a shepard pipes his flute,
Somewhere still the harper plays his strings,
And somewhere still a baby's cry disperses
In that song which every mother sings.

THIS MORNING YOU STOOD IN THE MARCH SUN

(Love Song)

This morning you stood in the March sun
Looking out the window at winter departing.
I do not know what kept you there so long,
In your hands a cup of herb tea steaming,

Or why you did not notice me in the hall
As I looked upon you, all of you, yet my
Gaze came to rest upon your nippled breast
For the sun came through your shirt, the why

Of optics I do not understand, in such a
Way as to transform the white of cotton into
The thinnest veil between breast and eye.
And they met. And stayed. Now all through

The many months of snow I heard you say
"I'm getting old! Look! More hair is grey,
Lines in my face, sagging breasts." You
Do not see them as I did in the sun today.

Not the same as twenty years ago they lie.
I see that and less firm now, two children
Nourished there. Girlish no more, they gain,
Well-used, well-kept, more in the eye of men.

ROVING

    I

Let us suppose
In this snow clogged dream
Of a rural winter night
We do not awake but seem

To rove the whither.

And let us suppose that
Our swirling, pointless
More than we can ever
Know, forces us to confess

And to come hither

Where godless winds do blow
Cold and soulless snow
Upon the bald, mute heads
Of the sitting, mumbling dead.

    II

Brown snakes slither

But not in folds of
Fallen snow where little
Creatures beg us to
Arise off our crinkled knees.

III

O rove the heather!
Rove, rove, rove
And it shall come a running,
Love shall come a running.

O rove the heather!
Rove, rove, rove
Where white flies the dove
And whiter flies our love.

Rove, rove, O roving
Until bleak night comes
When the earth's hinges creak
And an eery silence hums.

Come, come rove with me.
Rove, rove the heather!
Leave only when the moon beams sting
And you will leave me never.

BY BARN DOOR WAITS

I

By barn door waits
The black cat, its
Mouse unveiled, its
Bird in flight, cat
Patience perfect

As mammoth flakes
Of spring snow flop
Upon a world
Of sodden slumber still,
Still of numbed desire.

II

Hibernation:
From harsh despair,
From frustration,
From death desire,
From all is wrong
Desperation,

We tire to hear
Lamentations,
Jeremiah
Notwithstanding!

III

O mouse, O bird!
Patience perfect:
Of this you've heard.

IV

O flight of bird,
O rodent running;
Within our house
The world's at peace

While the cat still
Waits: the tense of
Patience perfect.
Our spring will come!

SPRING

Temptress Spring
Stirred Blazing Thoughts

I

Temptress spring stirred blazing thoughts
Of browning flesh enfolding meadow ponds
Splayed like phalanxed armies flanked,

Nubile sucklings clinging to the old orb's
Nurturing tit, thighs spread, hilly rumps,
Orchestrated chests riming chorded
Breaths in heating harmonies.

Down, down protracted corridors of expectation,
Wet and warm, come the harbingers.

II

But where are the envisaged girls cut from crave?
The pond is there, its polliwogs, its mottled trout,
Its swallows swooping over clover grass and spindly reed.

What source sends flaccid matriarchs of middle age,
Mortared slab on slab of greased up flesh, glutted in new
Swimming skirts of flower prints, bodices flooding under
High-pitched prate, chirruping chits posturing near?

III

From volcanic visions
Such travesty has sprung?
Deracinated dreams decay.

Uprooted, I waste,
Shriveling by the pond.
Etched upon pallid eye,
The water nymphs slick submerge.

Two Refrains

I
(From the girl's Song)

"Tomorrow we'll dance in the nude, boys!
 Tomorrow we'll dance for you.
 We will get all dressed up just to get undressed.
 It's tomorrow we'll dance for you!"

II
(From the boy's Song)

"It never happens.
 No! It never, ever happens.
 But it gives us something to wait for.
 Yeh! It gives us something to wait for."

Eat

I

Hunger on, on, all through each day,
The autobiography of eat we write
With bones from beef to leaves
Of tea, to rising in the middle night

For milk, for cake, to cleave
An appetite which expands us tight
Against our grieving skin, anchors
Of uncomely bags about our bones.

II

Hunger on, on, each day, at night.
Eating our way through time's wake
As if life were some dumb mistake
We must remake with

Spoon and fork, shoveling.
Meats rent by serrated knives,
We masticate our very lives
In an ever, ever eat

Of esophagus,
Intestines two,
And the
Press and pass

Of warm excrement
Against the spine.

Two Lines of Discontent

Two lines of discontent:
Too much sperm and cement!

Spring Storm Requiem

As fast as sprinters at the tape
Lead weighted snows
Of an April storm
Bring hand-hewn barns to heaps,

Crippling mountain farms
Left perched upon a crutch.
Unleashed waters leap
And cellars fill to boots, while

Fractured fences
Lie unnursed
Inciting uncharted tours
On mud-wrecked roads

Of panicky horses
Out-running homes.

Perspicacious Nature knows
What she is about,

I'm sure,
For we've been taught
The universe unrolls
According to an ordered plan!

There must be good,
Inscrutable, of course,
Beneath the good god's
Catastrophic tricks

When power lines look
Like spaghetti strands
And our trees
Like pick-up sticks.

Ars Poetica Again

(With apologies to Archibald MacLeish and Others)

I

I know how trends and
Fashions alter, it's
Part of history,
Those subtle changes in our arts,
Our speech and dress, our haute cuisine,
   And the way we see

Ourselves and relate
To what we were and
To that we'll someday be.
Also, I know what's "in" and "out"
In music, movies, and modes literary
   And therefore must ask

(Quickly admitting
I'm an amateur):
In that what passes
Now for the Muses verse with words
Lacking sound, sense, rhyme, and meter,
Where's the poetry?

II

Here's a recipe for poems
Should you wish to write your own tomes:

   Meter's passe
   And so are rhymes
   So just write prose
   On anything,
   Mundane or dull,
   Arithmetic,
   A broken egg,
   Even better
   An old receipt,
   And break it up
   In fragment lines,
   Some short, some long
   And then the end
   Of ART: title
   It and you're through!

It is a ruse and all know it
But who cares now you're a poet!

PILGRIM COMES HOME

I

"It was that bad?"
"It was that bad!"
  Need does reset
  A home regained.

11

Set! A to zed:
Some Scotch and fed
Starts to restore
What I adore

Of pigs, of sheep,
Of land vast as
Sea where sweet thee
Tolerates me.

The A, B, C's of Cyril's Holiday

(After Schopenhauer's "Die Welt als Wille und Vorstellung")*

> * Schopenhauer's major work is usually translated as "The World as Will and Idea"

A. World

The "Manual of Marriage and Morals"
Is left on the library shelf of the
Elmwood Heights
First Congregational Church

When their organist, Cyril, goes on holiday.
Once each year
Cyril gives his organ to other hands
And tells his wife

(She's a Stockbroker—
Their vacations never coincide)
That he's off to photograph the world;
Barren beaches of Bahamian shores

Or wild animals of Africa.
Cyril knows a waitress well.
He pays her travel fare
So he can share

SPRING

Her ebony jewels for two short weeks.

B. Will

He photographs
Her big brown boobs
He photographs
Her big bronze bum
He photographs
Her coal black bush.
How can Cyril's wife
Be so goddam dumb

To never even ask
To see his photographs?
She seems not to care at all

How Cyril uses space or time
As long as Cyril
Trims the grass

And vacuums out the hall.

C. Idea

Two short weeks is just too little time
To stock up on life.
Cyril's home again and
Now taking estimates
On an addition to his wife.

Daddy Disconsolate

I

Daddy? Who's the
Pretty lady
Who smartens up
My hair and takes

Me off to bed
And tucks me in
And brings me juice
And toast and where,

Daddy, O where
Did my mommy
Go? Will she be
Back to me? Who

Took her off in
That fancy car?
Will she come back
To me, Daddy?

II

Daddy? Why do
You crawl on hand
And knee like our
Doggy does? Why

Fiercely pitch your
Masticated
Stew on our lawn
At cock's crow dawn

Then sink into
Raglike heaps and
Sleep, half nude, on
The hard cold, cold

Kitchen floor? Where
Can my Mommy
Be, Daddy? And
Tell who is the

Lady sleeping
Where my Mommy
Slept? O where can
My Mommy be?

Will she return
To me? Who is
She calling me
Her "little dear,"

Daddy? O please
Will you answer
Me? I need to
Know. Who is she?

Splitting Wood in Spring

Splitting wood in spring
Makes damn good sense to
Those who know that new

Winter is waiting
Close behind the last
Drops of our melting

April snow. It is
Our old friends, who are
Old, who die more often

As life yields
Its
Brief proportions
Inexorably

To us. Swing with your
Muscles those tools that
Tell how force, like fire,

Is not yet ash in
White, dusty heaps, but
Battles with firm

Finalities which
Walk in winter's cold
and hoary shoes! Left

Right, left, right, stalking us,
Tracking ever faultlessly
From high mountain notch
To the thirsty jaw of the sea.

Deductions of a College Freshman

Am I my me to shed,
Like the snake who in dusty turning
Leaves its skin on the pasture's edge,
Under the weight of all this learning

Hung in the expanded heads
Within these ancient Ivy, brick walls?
This worming thought, written upon
August faces hanging in the polished halls,

Burrows into my dolesome mind.
It's just that all that I have been taught,
All those values, all the truths
Are daily stood like guilty men

And shot down dead before me.
There they lie and here I descry,
From Kennedy to Christ,
The unraveling of one, long lie.

Why weave it in the first place?
But the dead, used skin was not
The snake nor were these slogans mine.
So! What's left? Sex and Pot!

Burial of the Blonde Girl's Cat

(For Alice: 1974)

The spade shovel
sliced the gravel, scored, and pried
loose the stones.

Deeper grew the
rounding hole on the edge of the
ostinato

brook whose studied
indifference to the shovel's strike, off-pitch,
accompanied me.

He ran off
to find a wife, to make kittens,
she had said,

returning home
from our holiday, finding one cat
less at her

heels as she
here kitty kitty, here kitty kittied
her way to

the barn, milk
and kibble in the hands of her
daily chores

thirty times more
before the corner of my eye picked
out his dead

sleep under
the old duck bin in the watery
cellar of

the barn. She
fed above, thus had not seen his
fatherhood

rotting in
spring mire. Somewhere a furry feline
goddess knows

how or why.
The ossuary was a perfect fit for
what would soon

be but bones.
It was, I surmised, during arithmetic
when eight plus

miles north of
her ciphers, creeping out from the fall
of long blond hair

upon her desk, that an ancient barn for not
the first time

nor the last,
supervised subtraction. Her
sheepdog,

always until
now, at the tail's end of the racing tom

little watched
from his gravel road as a shovel
presided, the

funeral songs
sung by birds joyful death
did inspire.

Mensuration 1, 2, 3, or Something About Sady

     1.

The old Nanny's harangue is a song
Which harps like this:

   "Mismate, masturbate, misogyny"

But she gets paid for her work?
In this there is no hapless quirk
For her employer previously agreed
To a contract for her to earn her feed

Yet on and on she chants
That same damn old song:

   "Mismate, masturbate, misogyny"
   "Mismate, masturbate, misogyny"
   "Mismate, masturbate, misogyny".

Her bitch is with biology or with Zeus!
How much does the money matter?
Does she sneak her gripes to Sady,
The Spic and Span cleaning lady?

     2.

Now Mr. Medford has had three sons
By the mistress of the house
But all his fun, or so the
Gardiner tells Sady, comes
Out-of-town on week nights.

3.

From the city to the suburb,
From the suburb to the city:
A dollar commute every day, each way.

Poor Sady!
How does she sing . . .
And of what?

Excerpt from "The Good Friday Spell" of Wagner's *Parsifal*

(A version in American English)

Parsifal
How beautiful the meadow appears to me today.
Once before I came upon magical flowers
Whose tainted tendrils entwined my head
But never have I seen grasses, blossoms and flowers
So soft and delicate as these
Or with a fragrance so sweet and fresh
Which speaks so dearly to me.

Gurnemanz
That is Good Friday magic, my Lord!

Parsifal
Alas! That day of utmost grief!
When, it seems, everything that blooms,
Breaths, lives and is born again,
Should mourn, ah! and weep.

Gurnemanz
You see that it is not so.
Today the sinner's remorseful tears
Are a holy dew
Covering the flowery meadow

And causing it to flourish.
Now all creatures rejoice
At the evident presence of the Redeemer,
And dedicate their prayers to Him.
They cannot see the cross
So they look up upon a redeemed mankind,
Freed from all sin and dread,
Cleansed and saved by God's loving sacrifice.
Every blade of grass and flower in the meadow
Senses this,
For today all men walk gently
Just as God, with infinite patience,
Took pity on them and suffered for them.
On this day in piety
Man spares the flower with gentle step.
All creation give thanks
All that blooms and is mortal,
For today nature is absolved
And gains its innocence.

   Parsifal
Wie dünkt mich doch die Aue heut so schön! —
Wohl traf ich Wunderblumen an,
die bis zum Haupte süchtig mich umrankten;
doch sah ich nie so mild und zart
die Halme, Blüten und Blumen,
noch duftet' all so kindisch hold
und sprach so lieblich traut zu mir.

   Gurnemanz
Das ist . . . Karfreitagszauber, Herr!

   Parsifal
O wehe des höchsten Schmerzentags!
Da sollte, wähn' ich, was da blüht,
was atmet, lebt und wieder lebt,
nur trauern, ach! und weinen!

   Gurnemanz
Du siehst, das ist nicht so.

Des Sünders Reuetränen sind es,
die heut mit heil'gem Tau
beträufet Flur und Au':
der liess sie so gedeihen.
Nun freut sich alle Kreatur
auf des Erlösers holder Spur,
will ihr Gebet ihm weihen.
Ihn selbst am Kreuze kann sie nicht erschauen:
da blickt sie zum erlösten Menschen auf;
der fühlt sich frei von Sündenlast und Grauen,
durch Gottes Liebesopfer rein und heil.
Das merkt nun Halm und Blume auf den Auen,
dass heut des Menschen Fuss sie nicht zertritt,
doch wohl, wie Gott mit himmlischer Geduld
sich sein erbarmt' und für ihn litt,
der Mensch auch heut in frommer Huld
sie schont mit sanftem Schritt.
Das dankt dann alle Kreatur,
was all da blüht und bald erstirbt,
da die entsündigte Natur
heut ihren Unschuldstag erwirbt.

MAY

He placed her hand in his,
A smaller, whiter hand,
And walking past
Pines and birches, past
Maples paired with beech,
They to their clearing climbed,
Stopped, and upon wide worlds below
Of meadow and of woods,
Viewed, in a silence understood,
What purpose shared they know
Brought and held them there
Where as one yet each alone
In that desired or what one did dare,
Made of it a home.

The Figment

    Matin sun
    and
    Matin moon

The vast informing of our flowers by the bees,
The vernal throb attires our trees and
Forces helpless infidelities between relenting knees.

    Matin sun
    and
    Matin moon

The vast informing of our flowers by the bees,
In vernal throb swelling brown into the
Monumental green where forbidden lovers seize

    Unseen under
    A matin moon
    Only to squirm

A little in the vigilant morning sun.

First Vignette from a Nearby Village

    (Tully and Kim)

The Joneses,
Tully and Kimberly,
Married a baker's dozen,
Have rooms of time
Still to pass through,
Empty door mazes
Of night on night.

They sleep in one
(A portion of their home)

Where Tully left for Kimberly,
By the bed-side lamp,
This love-brimming poem:

"Goodnight my Love"

All that talk about poor, wretched golf widows
I have heard it all too many times before.
While each night you glean TV, half sunk in sleep,
I could have seduced your friends or bought a whore.

And he went to sleep.

Choired peepers
Chant canticles
Of spring in the
Meadow pond through
Repressing fingers
Of night's bent gnome.

Valley sleepers,
Wine sopped,
Chill curled,
Their obliterated agonies
Sentinels of empty hands
Passed heading home.

Eyes of Argus
Looking into night,
Do you never speak?
Cosmic voyeur

Employed I am
To see what is concealed:
Poor Tully jacking off
And the dt's of sots.

Condone kismet.
She has no cull,
Noon to noon.

Wings out,
If you have a pair!
But a sot and Tully
Do not.

Second Vignette from a Nearby Village

    Time: May 21, 1971, 10:15 PM
    Place: The living room of Bill and Barb Hopkins,
            married thirty years ago today.

(The Reflections of Bill)

Another year has passed and though
I had not noticed until now you have
Changed a bit (and so have I) and
Aphrodite does not come to visit you
As much anymore yet you still look
Rather pretty sitting there on the floor,
Your uncombed hair presiding over
Diaphanous powder blue peignoir.

Your feet are bare, I like that!
A sign warm spring has come again,
But here we sit. A glance. No words
Except your "Well, I guess I am ready for
Sleep." And that is it for another night.

Together, off we will go to practice and
To prepare to perfect ourselves for
That one night, not too long from now,
When we strut a minor part on the
Stage of unalterable reclamations.

Senta for the Dutchman Sang

(22 May: Richard Wagner's Birthday)

I

Senta for the Dutchman sang
"Hier steh' ich treu Dir bis zum Tod"*
And plunged to death in but one kind
Of love. There are others.

II

Eureka!
May Queen Harry, this Maytide.
Post maypop to northern clime, pronto.

Mayest thou,
Gymnosophists, jiggle thy genitals
Around the hawthorne pole

Of May?
Hetaerism of bare bums
Soon to squash stinking camomile

In rimed hammerings.

*"Here I stand, faithful to you until death." The final line of Wagner's "The Flying Dutchman" is sung by Senta.

Image

(Nine year old Thoroughbred)

Centuries of a single blood
Surges in swelled nostrils flying
Over farm and over fields
Half touched by hooves whose heart
Sprung leaps defray dreaded dying
In courser vaults of Sickle yields
Which cut and cull mere things apart:

SPRING

An isolated whinnying;
Long, dropping sighs befalling silence.

I Visit Bob

(A Ditty No Less Serious)

I visit Bob
Every week, a
Habit I much
Approve, as year
Adds upon year.

"Build us a drink,"
He says, as I
Come through the door,
For next the sink
Our favorite
Special whiskey
Is beckoning
(And nuts for me).

The weekly toast,
"Cheers," we say and
All about the
Whole wide world we
Go, yet never,
Ever leave our
Chairs, conversing
Of music, of
The books we've read,
Wodehouse, Rumpole,
And Conan Doyle.

We talk of the
Living and we speak
Of the dead who
We much admire;

Mark Twain, of course,
And Oliver
Wendall Holmes. We
Laugh, jibe, and mock
Ever-present
Human Folly

("Tutto nel mondo e' burla")* *From Verdi's *Falstaff* ("The whole world is but a joke")

And chastise the
Poor hollow men

("Headpiece stuffed with straw,")** **From T.S. Eliot's *The Hollow Men*

We play with words
Of languages,
Recall renowns
Of Crimson gowns
In Cambridge town:
That's what we do
But stop short of
Religion, that
Progenitor
Of most war! Of
Economics
Nary a word.
It's such a waste
(And bad taste, too).

Nor chat about
Politics which
Makes us sick, the
Power hungry
Baffoons. Thoughtful
Men do not waste
Words today on
Ego deeds or
The First Lady's
Dress or the rest
Of that trite mess.

"Buy another,"
  Bob suggests. While
  The bottle pours
  Dogs bark sharply
  Out-of-doors, birds
  Sing the setting
  Sun which slowly
  Slides away as
  Night takes the light
  From day as two
  Old friends pass hours
  Doing best what
  Best they do, that
  Thinking, talking
  And downing of
  A drink or two . . .

  Or three. Or three!

  Friends and whiskey
  Regularly. What
  Could be better
  In all kinds of
  Weather, I ask,
  Than to pass time
  With drinks and speech
  We deem sublime
  Writ forever,
  Though odd of rhyme,
  In verse clever

  Enough for us!

The Brook

Swollen with melted snow, inflamed,
Battering its bounds like a boy's heart
Idling bat and ball for love, the brook
Burns in its festival of spring. Departs

By thumping wings? Off he flies
To the promised land. Sunk well
Into her sumptuous back, flexed thighs
Grip his sorrel mare. To nearby hell

She pounds the dirt in two. "Look!
I see him coming." And now he's by,
His long hair strutting the wind
And taking blue from the sky.

O yes: the brook. I walked from the
House the few steps to where I put
Up the dam, looked to the hill,
And watched the water cascade down. Still,

So stupidly still, I stood, so tired,
Still but for that twitch in my eye.
Long August was in my mind for I saw
My brook lie down, wizened, and die

To a trickle, bumping over stones
Glimmering in the sun, its turgid
Flow spent in another hour. "Hey!
Ride, boy, ride!" Ah, surely he knew

That she lay hid by the larch of the meadow
gate. But does he know how
Soon it's late and that upon his strewn
Out face he'll look to see it slip

From under him in the
Coursing of a brook.

Some Spirit Minus Matter

Hundreds of lilac towers
Of lavender, of purple, of white,
Encircling bowers
About a grey old house,
Issue zephyred fragrances
In and out all day, all night

Until flowers fade
And die away
And the fragrance gone
And yet in memory
It trails on,

The scent remains,
The perfumes lingering on
And Lilies of the Valley;
Oh! The Lilies of the Valley.

SUMMER

Rummage Sale

I

His own heart he
Rummaged keenly
To find many
Raiments of loves
Some forgotten
Some repressed some
Simply over
Without remorse

II

The summer sale
At church was his
Intent there to
Peddle remains
Of passion spent
And remnants of
Tenderness which
Still had some worth

III

Off he went his
Particles snug
In his grasp it
Was not money
He was gleaning
He so sorely
Had a need to
Empty his heart

IV

Everything sold
His walk back home
Was driven by

A heart in which
Only blood and
A muscle reigned
How unburdened
Was his sprite gait

      V

How the church had
Hoped to hold him
How the lady
With the tags had
Tried to break his
Shield but he left
With much less than
They intended

      VI

Not even God
Gained his ear for
Here was a man
Subject to his
Own cleansing the
Object of his
Own salvation
He was alone

      VII

As he walked
No breezes blew
To refresh his
Brow no birds sang
To his happy songs
But how he sang
His opera of
Expurgation

VIII

Home again he
Warmed his soup
Ate fiddled out
A tune or two
Stared into the
Emptiness of
Nothing else to
Do and retired

RILKE'S ARCHAIC TORSO OF APOLLO

(A version in American English)

We know not his missing head,
wherein the eyes did age. But
his torso still glows like a candelabrum
in which his countenance, restored therein,

is preserved and shines forth. Were it not so the curved
breast could not blind you, and in the gentle turn
of the loins a smile could not reach
to that middle, which carried the genitals.

Were it not so this stone, mutilated and short,
would stand under the clear sloped shoulders
and would not glisten like the coats on beasts of prey;

nor burst out of its borders
like a star; for there is no place
which does not see you. You must change your life.

ARCHAÏSCHER TORSO APOLLOS

by Rainer Maria Rilke

Wir kannten nicht sein unerhörtes Haupt,

darin die Augenäpfel reiften. Aber
sein Torso glüht noch wie ein Kandelaber,
in dem sein Schauen, nur zurückgeschraubt,

sich hält und glänzt. Sonst könnte nicht der Bug
der Brust dich blenden, und im leisen Drehen
der Lenden könnte nicht ein Lächeln gehen
zu jener Mitte, die die Zeugung trug.

Sonst stünde dieser Stein entstellt und kurz
unter der Schultern durchsichtigem Sturz
und flimmerte nicht so wie Raubtierfelle;

und bräche nicht aus allen seinen Rändern
aus wie ein Stern: denn da ist keine Stelle,
die dich nicht sieht. Du musst dein Leben ändern.

Six Meditations from a Sheepdog's Reveries

One

"Take care of the farm,"
Said they, in
Exodus

And left me alone a long
And lonely
Week.

Two

The moon returns and goes.
Balls of snow amass to my
Shaggy clothes.
Spring mud! Flies to bite!

Wind-stung leaves of fall
To chase. The moon returns

And goes.
Again the long and lonely snows.

Three

My pond of twenty trout
Or more
I drink
How many deer
Barked
From fruit-filled apple boughs
How many mares
Gathered
For their grass and grain
How many minutes
Enervate
In pedomorphic play
How many nights
Sharply called at 3 AM
To cease conversing with
The black Labrador half mile away
How many cats
Sent
To barn rafters running
How many sheep
Sprung
From their grazing.

Four

They mete and dole me equal laws [1]
I love, they love, we love
Canine connubial conjugations
Down in younder green field
There lies a Knight slain under his shield. [2]
Let us now consider the infinitive "to dog."
His hounds they lie down at his feete,
So well they can their master keepe [3]
School's out after this last allusion when
Death and darkness in that instant closed

1. "I mete and dole unequal laws..." "Ulysses" by Tennyson.

2 & 3. From "The Three Ravens" 17th Century English Ballad.

*The eyes of Argos, who had seen his
Master after twenty years.*[4]

    Five

Dyslexia?
We dogs must undo
That ancient faith
They ascribe to

As we reveal
The reversal
Needed in an
Elemental word.
God! How absurd.

Turn G-O-D around
To make it right:
With D-O-G
They'll see the light!

    Six

Moon and brook!
We are three
Of the farm, comingled
In our blood and in our
bone.

My watch
I'll keep,
Moon, your shining,
You, cold waters,

On the run.

---

4. From Book XVII of
The Odyssey by Homer.

The Youths

"Long about the meadow pond
  Long-limbed lovers met curt time
  And wish what I may, old time
  Wish, could I, my love meet mine.

"The sleep of pastures, sleep of barns,
  The ram and ewes awake to love
  Yet we, alone, so vast alone,
  Scrutinize the sky above

"For one touch of torrent time,
  Banging rural brooks alive,
  To grant long-limbed love
  That fateful dive

"Into dire need heaping proof
  Upon the soil of both our lives.
  So what are we to do? What do we do?"
  "Hush! Just live our love until it's through."

Poseidon with His Trident

(After a Greek, red-figured vase of the 4th Century B.C.)

I

Trident thrusting.
Nothing,
if measured by the prick of Poseidon

aroused by brave
soft flesh under dress of
deep-breasted Gaea.

Driven to his weakening knee.
listing on his spear,
uncocked,

aegis blanketing condensing back,
death inching toward his maw,
Polybotes

is dressed for war.
Earth,
nude Poseidon,
will intercede the shaking loins
of the jealous, copulating sea.

      11

On this grey morn of June, humid and hot,
behind hills in foggy locks, the risen sun
stands hid

and sheds a dull ray down this farm where, still
in antique bed, I turn from sleep to raise a query:

    Sex plays such a crucial role in
    the interpreting above, did you,
    shepherd friend, compensate for
    lack of love?

Sex and love are not the same, as
surely you ought to know. Of love there is some,
but of sex, lots. How else, I ask, did
living forms come to be

if gods of Greece
did not descend and wedge between mere mortal knees?
Sex and war: the parents of us all. The eternal decree,
unless, of course, you subscribe to that theory of the sea.

Do you believe in such fairy tales?
Pagan gods as true? You

do believe in such fairytales!

O yes, O yes I do do do!

III

Iambic pentameter,
trochee, trimeter, tetrameter all a jumble:
this verse is mere mumble
of ametrical mouths.

You must be on pension
if you have time for scansion.

Back now
to the vase
where verse is free:
back to the muscly

sea in
contoured lines
drawn upon a Grecian vase

which once held wine
next cheese.

IV

More beautiful by far than a Grecian vase,
My lady, curved and white, my love, so wise,
Holds me, debased, in her complete despise.
Die I my only death could I but reflect
    (please turn her face),
Like Pekin ducks upon a reposed summer pond,
In those algid, tearless, sea-blue eyes.

V

Ah!
Stop this mutilation of

your futile imitation of
Petrarchan convention of

Forget her face,
stick to your vase,
and drink your Goddamn wine!

TETRAD

(Of a Summer Day)

I

Intermediaries
Must sing for

Those throats by
Promises choked:

But the flowers bloom.

II

Black mare and
Strawberry roan,

Rusted chains of
Fixing fences:

The black flies bite.

III

Bend to drink,
Like a dog,

Water from the
Swirling brook:

The sun is hot.

IV

The ducks depart;
A frog leaps.

They all take
Time away:

The half moon rises.

The Water in the Holy Stream

The water in the holy stream,
Pure as the pine is green,
Runs by the flowering banks.
Birds high in the sky reaching
Maple boughs sing sweet songs.

As he walks by
His dark and spotted soul
Hangs out,
Flapping behind him
In the rain-riddled wind.

West Coast of Ireland

I

Consonants cluster
Ever so gently in an Irish throat.
Speak the old tongues
Like pre-historic relic runes

The tunes of so much music in we
Who hear wind songs
Where sheep roam free,

We who hear more than clarion bongs
When ancient church bells ring
A Celtic peasantry
From stony huts next the sea

And in some pagan sacred way
Seems fast seducing me.

    II

I walk the throw down to the sea,
Oh, how much water can there be,
Oh, how I wish for sails for me.

I walk the throw down to the sea
And watch the moon dance on water
And sing with my mandolin

Songs of farewell,
Ballads of love and laughter,
The toasts whiskey brings,
And a moon dancing on water.

    III

As the bells clang over water
I respond without a word
Knowing that in an Irish silence
All has been said and heard.

THE ODD JOB NEIGHBOR

Sixty years before I stepped upon these hills,
He hiked, hunted, and hayed them down,
And when I came
He helped,

The odd job neighbor,

Teaching, without intent,
Three-fourths a century
Of experience.

How he hopped in laughter, quick to tease,
Yet terse, many-handed in his work,
Never a no to a need

Until one sudden day, I do not know,
Death came to him and said, "I'll walk in
You a while before
We go,"

And stole the trout from his finger tips,
Withdrew the sun-burst from his eye, and
Spread dry pallor
Upon his lips!

He grew ten years in one
Toward dust.

Green Growing Fierce in Force

    I

  Green growing fierce in force
"Snip, snip," the shears retort
  Along the fieldstone garden wall,
"Snip, snip," the shears retort

  Bearing up a shedded skin,
  Warped filmy jaws, translucent eye,
  A lesser half, this residue, this
  Ghostly replica of quick slithering

  Under steps, jarring paces headed home.
  Green growing, green growing,
  We attempt to tame what some distant

Spring will claim in a long sleep.

11

I start.
The nesting swallows
Dart
And ride the ether blue
Above.

More than this,
This Monday morning fragment
Of mountain summer;
More than this.

There is much more in this
Human puppet show stage-bound by
Green growing, green growing,
Valley forest, valley field
Much more than grassing snakes
Or pairing swollows
Yet today I only note

Green growing,
Shedded skin slither underfoot,
And sky perfecting flight for

Half the summer has gone away
Half the summer it is gone
Half the summer has gone away
And one assembles memories.

WITNESS THE WORDS OF
ONE WITHOUT

"Home again, Gulliver
 Conversed with his horses
 Two hours everyday.

Did he do all the
Talking while they
Munched away their hay?

I tried to talk to my
Team as they nibbled
Summer grasses and

Spilled their steaming turds
And I tell you quite honestly
They never said one word."

"Never said a word," I amended,
"Nonsense! You don't know how to listen
 Or surely you would have comprehended!"

ON LOOKING FOR CAROLYN

   *(A poem for a 50th birthday of a neighbor
   who loves music)*

Resounding ever
From the Robbins house
Cantatas by Bach
Or songs of Strauss
Or symphonies by William Byrd
Leaves my knocking completely unheard.

"Carolyn, O Carolyn," I raise my voice
 But it's obscured by chorales of Boyce.
"Carolyn, O Carolyn," I assert
 And who do I get? Schubert!
 And when I try once again
 There's the Ode of Beethoven.

Now where can she be?
I hear Stravinsky,
I know she's home

But all I find is Mendelssohn
Or a Brahms quartet
Or a Haydn mass
To occupy my impasse.

I try the barn
Where noise is heard.
It's not Carolyn
But some Schönberg
Twelve-tone scales
Which I deemed were
Feeding pails.
Ah! The garden, perhaps?
Music there is by Sir Arnold Bax.
Throwing hay to the stock?
That's a suite by Ernest Bloch.

"Enough of this,"
I complain
To harmonies
Of Arthur Bliss.
"I give up;
Time to depart,"
To *Zaïde*
By Mozart.
I start my car
And drive away
But O mercy, O me,
Vivaldi, Bellini,
Donizetti, Puccini,
The joke's on me.

She's been home all along
From Verdi's "Requiem" to Wagner's song
Gleefully spending her very last dollar
Ordering everything, absolutely everything,

Of Gustav Mahler!

SUMMER

Song of Farewell

(From "Nova Scotia Quartet")

Sun circular sea licked rock,
Gigantic under web of hermetic
Gull, circumspect, mocking
Great gods in distress

With cries of balding men
Passing kidney stones.

Barren bleak land oh,
Broil my brain to
Black char dust,
Blown away swolled

By the old salt sea.

Mordicai "Pistachio" Mumford's Poetry Sampler

"Rain on wild roses expunges."
"It what?"
"Expunges!"
"Expunges what?"
"It expunges the stinging sun,
 Deceitful men, the greeds of women,
 And obnoxious children."

Rain on the metal roofs
Of rural village homes clatters comfortably.

Duck feathers, wet.
Duck feathers wheeling
In the rain wet wind.
The feathers of
White Pekin ducks

SUMMER

Flutter in my scrubbed out skull
Walking its way in the spate.
My sodden hairs, a few remain,
Flush with my bony pate,
Are wetter than the feathers.
Do you see the feathers
Tossed and turned in my mind?

The debouched ducks, where have they gone?
The wind has sallied on.
The rain sinks through the
Happy sward,
Heading home.

Do you see the feathers?
White as the puffy clouds
They lie scattered on the ground
Lolling on the supine grass
Warming in the gentle heat of a
Rinsed-off sun.

"HE WHO ONCE THE BARNYARD RULED"

(After an etching by John Paulus Semple)

He who once the barnyard ruled,
With curved bill,
With curved claws,
Lies still, unfletched.
The boy stretched its neck;
Mere matter for our maw.

He who once the barnyard ruled,
O bird, O boy:
How you two grew
To men to die
As generations
Pass like suns turning through

Your descendents eye.
Egg and sperm
To a naked bird
Stewing in a pot.

Egg and sperm
To ashes in an urn.

BALLAD OF HANNAH THE HITCHHIKER

(Quid pro quo or Tit for Tat)

It was
Only
A summer
Filled with the fucks

Of the
Far away
Places of
Cross country trucks

Where
People live
Their almost
Good

And
Never heard
Of
Lives.

A MEDIEVAL ROMANCE

(The Musician)

I

Do you hear the mixolydian mode
In my prelude
Or have the rogues you rode
In wanton turpitude
Sired such guilt you cannot
Attend to the music
Which I wrote for you, you sot,
You egocentric
Bitch? Could you even feel
Remorse?

II

Concentric
Circles, dispersing, conceal
The submarine tricks
Which the universe perpetrates upon
Our pauperous souls.
Those able-bodied men in bon voyage
With you, you open-holed
Big breasted whore,
You think I know not,
Once out the door,
Your whereabouts? Fraught
With green of envy, volcanic
Hate bubbling *For I'm sick
At the heart and I fain wad lie
Down** to a harmonic
Chord and die
Than sing again for you.

* From the poem "Lord Randal" (Anonymous)

III

Concentric circles, dispersing,
Conceal the submarine

Tricks which the universe perpetrates
Upon our poor, lean souls.

The ship trails on. You have
Grown obese and old
And sleep alone. A slow
Wake runs off into the gold

Waves of dusk
While I, making a new song,
Sail home, warm wind upon my back.

A Modern Romance

(Ditty in a Minor Key)

As musicians play,
Dancing girls display
Nipples and pubic hair.
But they don't care

That they are nude!
While leering men
Drink their beers
And nibble food,

They get paid!
The leering men dream
Of getting laid
But their night ends

Unadventurously
With a sleazy dance
In a minor key.

Two Excerpts from
"The Isagogics of Joshua Winters"

I

DOUCE DAME

(After Guillaum de Machaut: c. 1300–1377)

*"Douce dame jolie,
pour Dieu ne penses mie
que nulle ait signourie
seur moy fors vous soulement."*

*("Milady sweet and fair,
By Heaven I declare,
To nothing do I bear
Allegiance save to thee.")*

Douce dame,
Seated beneath tall poles of
Fast, free revelry,
You look long in your mirror on anxious
Love.

Douce dame,
Unicorn half mounted upon your knee,
Fertile rabbits float
Upon a tapestry of medieval
Love.

Douce dame,
Creatures all are we,
Biped, quadriped,
Partaking in unfettered feasts of
Love.

Douce dame,
So pretty, sweet, so fair, so

Ready now with brocaded gown so
Lowered down for

Love.

  II

 EIGHT LINES

 (After Psalm 103)

Rides the wine
Eagle young
Above green rooted grass.
See them transform to dust

The branches
Of the aged vine;
Fruit born for
But fire a fire.

Gaudeamus

 ("in flagrante delicto")

Marion is married
And Edward engaged.
Her husband's furious;
His fiance's enraged

For they discovered
That very moment

When Edward had
A decided upright bent
Aimed precisely
At Marion's fundament!

An Ode for Our Time

(For Sam Sanders)

Poor Sam!
He demands excellence
For his recompense.
Surely! Remiss were
His early scholars
Not to school in him
An insatiable yen
For fame and dollars.

Two Fragments from Summertime

I
Summer Afternoon

("Summer afternoon . . . the two most beautiful
  words in the English language."
                              – Henry James)

Bluer than the sky was blue
An Indigo Bunting turned
Above field flower grasses flew
Their sympathies narrowly concerned
Old shepherd's crook thrushes note
Breasts pumping in his palms
Love's language snagging in their throat.

II
Summer Night

("Sound loves to revel in a summer night."
                              – Edgar Allen Poe)

Fireflies heat lightening
Excerpts from the moon

In cloudy flight
Of deep embrace face on face
They will be sleeping soon

Under rain rusted roof
A summer night
Edges toward contentment
Holding lovers tight

They who pace their older selves
Duets sung in unison
Dissolution under sheets
When all else is done

A dog pants
Brooks rap their rocks
In muffled moans

Swedish Ivy from an old porch
Hangs and sways in a breeze.

BURIAL GROUND

The August afternoon,
High on the village hill,
Stood still: time ceasing
And space resigned to limits.

The church of clapboards white
And rightly spired, stood rooted
To the land like elm and maple
Sentries along the road.

Like people the cold stones
In their time tilted rows, stood
On the rolling lot, with their names
Scratched upon their granite faces.

Not a single creature showed in
The hot summer sun as we drove
Past and then again and then saw
The April mud devour

A Parson and parishioners,
Long-legged men attired in black,
Ladies hidden by their bonnets,
Some children in their arms,

Some children lost in the six inch
Mire of mud trudging to the
Snorting horses fidgeting by
The road, almost shaking the old

Buggies from their backs, draining
The cold, sharp rain down their
Sculpted legs into the muck
Sunk hocks and hooves.

And home. Home to hill
Strung farms and fires
With one less to break the
Ground in May they are now

Each their own stone, hung
On the earth's sod face,
Reminding every passerby
Of their fate and where it goes.

PERHAPS SPIRIT CAN EXCEED MATTER

(In Memory Of My Father: Ralston Fox Smith, Jr.)

Prologue

Porgy on his goatcart inches toward Bess, he loves;
King Arthur on his barge drifts to his destiny;

A Knight answering a plea journeys long,
Gliding in his boat drawn by a swan with golden
Chain, while we, transfixed, must transcend
    mere imagery
To ascertain what urge says to strive or to submit.

    Part One: The Swan Boat

"Ein Schwan zieht einen Nachen dort heran!
*Ein Ritter drin hoch aufgerichtet steht!"**
               – From Wagner's *Lohengrin*

The swan flutes a clarion song
Along obscure waters of
The Scheldt

As a Knight answers Elsa's plea
With a self-centered love that
Cannot

Endure. Dire schism, Justified
Curiosity. "Dear swan! Come
Back," sounds

The Knight's golden horn; "Return
Us upon the dark and swirling stream to
A home

Far from the madness I conceived."
Can happiness be uttered in
Silence?

Sometimes silence does something say;
Some other times we must pay
With words

And then to walk forth with love,
To float upon a stream like
A swan,

*"A swan is towing a boat here! A knight is standing in it."

SUMMER

To make a song to be sung,
To come as an equal, not
As king,

For all in the end resolves
In silence, be it human or of
A swan.

   Part Two: The Goat Cart

    Porgy
"Won't nobody bring my goat?"

    All
"Where you goin', Porgy?"

    Porgy
"Ain't you say Bess gone to Noo York?
Dat's where I goin', I gotta be wid Bess."
          – From Gershwin's *Porgy and Bess*

As Porgy's goat cart crossed the Carolina line,
Heading northward to New York City, a lone grey cat
Commenced trotting at his side, mewing, the dark, deep
Eyes fixed on Porgy's smile until a great, brown hand
Swung down, gently took the cat, and raised it onto
A lap where soon it was all in sleep lulled by the slow
Rhythmic roll over the road and by the warm bass
Of Porgy's songs; ever northward, past fields of corn
To the ocean's shore, to the throbbing masses door.

  "Foolish, wonderful Porgy! Whatever made
    You think you could find your Bess?"

"A faith bigger than any thought brought me!"

"But you had to search so long."

"I always had my hope."

SUMMER

"I love you, Porgy."

"I love you, Bess."

Upon the old settee the cat lept, arched its
Back, stretched, and settled next the lame man's knee.

   Part Three: The Barge

"Then murmur'd Arthur 'Place me in the barge.'"
              – From Alfred, Lord Tennyson's *Idylls of the King*

Arthur in his bed upon the barge floated on the
River's spine, his life left behind him in those faint
Episodes of long, complicated, half-remembered dreams.
The past now yields to dragonflies liting on the prow,
To bees fliting bloom to bloom all along the shore,
To butterflies in bouncing flight, to waves lapping
On the hull their dolorous, repetitive dull
Resound. The supine King cannot see the water-
Snake bisect the dispersing wake of the barge as
It journeys toward the sea as eye-level rushes bend
And sway in a mesmerizing dance as old eyes
Close and open and then shut with the end of day.

The barge moves against the stars, following hoots
Of an owl as Arthur awakens to the dark till
Slowly, slowly a great curtain of light makes its
Way across the sky. He hears the water's rush,
Bleating goats far on the shore, he hears, too, gentle
Chatterings as the wind gusts in leafy boughs which
Overhang the stream and wave as he slips by in those
Drifting, mixing fragments of the far-off dreaming
Of great deeds and love decayed as the sun stares him
Eye to eye, the blank blue sky without a fleece of
Cloud, a great empty stage. His final scene begins:
Etched on bare blue, in soaring flight, an eagle's wings.

SUMMER

Epilogue

More mysterious travel
Could be told but ends

With Sali and Vrenchen,
Young lovers of rival families
Fighting for land to which
The eccentric Dark Fiddler
Is the rightful heir.

Repudiated by all they have
But each the other
And together they respond
To a call:

"How the dreaming silent flood,
  Slowly gliding, seems to call us"*

*From Delius'
"A Village Romeo and Juliet"

They, like Arthur, set adrift
Upon a barge and quickly pulled its plug,
And settled in a bed of hay,
Their marriage bed,
For rapture brief
And long repose
As they sank through
Water dark and deep
To disappear.

What once was
Is no more.

Across the drifting stream
Fiddle tunes fade and
Strands of hay float
Idly away.

All else is gone
But their story.

SUMMER

FALL

How Fast Fall Falls

How fast fall falls
Upon these northland hills,
Their green valley
Metamorphosis ablaze

With flames of ardent
Lover's lust. How fast
Fall falls upon
Green leaf of May.

Place some measure next
Our feeble thrusts,
Our fantasies,
Our wonderings.

But such detracts
As cold winds
Carry leaves away
In senseless swirls.

How we cipher, how
Subtract, and much
Bemoan could have
Been. How fast fall

Falls upon
Green leaf of May.
How quickly we come;
How fast we go away.

To Christmas Cove

(A birthday poem from a birthday trip for Joanne)

I

I have not words
to reproduce moves of
a flock of birds
locked in flight,

their sixty wings
swinging as one
within inviolate
border rim,

yet each to
instinct and whim
uncharted sails
on the high thin

sea of grey
autumn day, a
fading drove
driving as one.

I have not words
to fly the birds.
Arthritic elm
bare above the

country road,
grey bones, finger
and limb, above
the shadeless house

where, like the
four last songs of Strauss,
hydrangeas swell
and over-flow.

In them I see
the Great War's men
white and ruddy brown
in slow motion

tumble down to death
as if scheduled
in some ritual
tribal dance.

    I I

A Christmas day
in centuries past
a rust-free anchor hit
the rocky floor

and bit the Captain's ship
against the flooding flow
in Christmas Cove. We
sit now in coveside chairs

and I see where
they offered prayers
upon the knee-bent deck
ghosting there

in our September sun
where crow and gull
caw and cry
together flying

for the morsels
drying on the
ebb tide shore:
The perfume rose.

III

Off your breasts
fuller than fantasies
round and real
the perfume rose

like fragile mists unfixing
from Poseidon's brow.
Back roads home
through mountain passes

ups and downs
some ferns already brown.
Ancient and proud
stand fences of stone

above finite grasses.
We pass quiet and close.
I think of hydrangeas
of birds in flight

of rise and fall
of perfumed breasts
of fin de siècle
all around

everywhere but here
for to us it seems
this day there
comes another.

Two Songs

I

(The father's song)

Only three miles to go
To eternity.

Only three miles to go
To eternity.

I've got but three miles to go
To eternity.

What will I do
When I am there?

O what will I do
When I am there,

O what will I do
When I am there?

I've got but three miles to go
To eternity.

What will I do
When I get there?

II

(The child's song)

Daddy's getting old and tired,
Daddy's almost gone.
Daddy's getting old and tired,
Poor man's almost gone.

Daddy's getting old and tired,

Daddy's almost gone,
Mommy's busy out in back
Diggin' a hole in the lawn.

It isn't sad or funny.
He never made much money.
Poor man's so old, so tired,
Poor man's almost gone.

Indian Summer

The gift of Indian Summer
   In a long bark canoe
Paddling the quiet evening
   Only a loon and you.

   Only a loon and you
And the little kit foxes
   Nipping at the water.

Ars Apologia in Sonata Form

Necessary pecks and patches
(food and cloth)
and art ringing senses
like fortress bells bonging victory
over waves and blood drenched grasses.

Necessary pecks and patches
(food and cloth)
and art ringing senses
like fortress bells bonging victories
over waves and blood drenched grasses.

The notes read
the rhythms kept

the holes fingered speedily
the old recorder sings

more sweetly than
medieval voices,
Christ imbued.
The peasants song

swallows thoughts and dreams
as if one process of the brain,
awake or in its sleep, spins still
disjointed semblances,

draping them like
spider webs throughout
the ceilings of our mind,
many stories where unread volumes

in foreign tongues
uncataloged are shelved.
Hear the song:
Feel the song!

Go with it
to the end
and stay. The tunes
they tell our blood to run
like lovers long in August hay.

Aspen shrinks the meadow down,
waves still rock
they stony shore while art
wrings out what sense is left
as if disproving some theorem or more.

Necessary pecks and patches
(food and cloth)
and art ringing senses
like fortress bells bonging victory
over waves and blood drenched grasses.

FALL

I'll Climb to Old Red's Grave

I

I'll climb to old Red's grave
When I'm convinced he's under ground.
He's been busy almost a year;
I haven't seen him since apple getting

Yet for years he's always made his rounds
To start a car or pump, splice wires,
Mortar stone, plaster, paint, or plant,
Speaking gently to the seeds.

Hear him talking with our children,
Hear his home-made names for them,
For they were his too, for
He had none,
And so are we,
Children to this father of us all, and they are too.

See his stroking hands
Speak to horse, to cow,
To cats, dogs, ducks,
With scarcely a word emitting from
Those gentle, smiling lips of
This linguist of our land whose
Fist full of bread calls up
The trout.

II

I'll climb the path toward old Red's grave
To place some flowers near
But not until I'm sure he's there
And not off boiling at his still
Or out jacking deer.

I'll go to old Red's stone
Only when I know he's there

To watch our hills
Unfolding at his feet.

On Making Love

A New Testament Exegesis

I

("... the lust of our flesh, fulfilling the desires of the flesh ..." Ep. 2.3)

He nibbled
Her nipples
Erotically.

She stroked
His chest
Caressingly.

They converged,
Merged, surged,
And purged

Vagina and verge

Then submerged
In sleep
Harmonically.

II

("And they sang a new song ..." Rev. 5.9)

Examine now what you just read
Above about making love
And note how it is really
An ode to music more than

The sex it purports to laud.
Detect the major keys, shifts
Into a minor mode, and
No cacophonies (he did
Not bite her nor did she scratch
Him). Notice, too, the Whole rest
Before arpeggios swell,
Explode, and diminish to
Pianissimo close, the
Duet in unison sung,
Now only silence left to
Resound persistently in
Our ears, that ever fading

Vibration upon old gears
Which grind us from one place to
Another, from here to there,
Or from start to stop, even
More from beginnings to that
Termination when there is
No more, that certain ending
Of love, of song, of all things.

III

("O thou of little faith, wherefore didst thou doubt?"
— Math. 14.31)

Were you taken
In by that bit
About a love
Lyric meter
With rhyme being
Symbolic for
Music meanings?

IV

("This is my commandment, that ye love one another..."
– John 15.12)

They stirred.
Their lips met
And all heard
The clash,

And the mashing of breast on breast,

And the
Bongs of bodies banging
And the high rapturous
Ejaculation
Of their passion song:

   "Oh, God."
   "Oh, God!"

Those six seconds,
Or eight,
Of our most holy praise,
Those spare sacred seconds
When two parts become one
When mortals become
God and Goddess entwined

   Apotheosis

Praising each the other's name

   "Oh God, Oh God"

Theist and atheist alike
Which, of course, may some befuddle
But human life sometimes is
A mean or merry muddle

And people can be pretty silly
And some people are just dumb.

But whatever:
The loving sure is fun!

Arthur King's Hills

None of us in the search
Knew the hills like he who

Had gamboled there as a boy
Building broken-branch forts

Or, while seated on the ledge
Ruptured ground, pulled thoughts

From a mad and tossing stream
To dissect, amend, discard or follow

To some logical end.
Hunting these hills his first

Squirrel fell under its scrawny
Tail and there, as well, ground-hogs

And coons commenced their limp
Journey to the tottering barn.

And one chilled November morning,
A Saturday, he stood with his

Shoulders high, though he was not
Really very tall, among the

Congratulating men who numbered six
Points in all of his very first buck,

Gutted, registered, and hanging before
Noon. It was his eleventh year,

Six years ago. Yes, six years
Ago and more often in that time

He has just gone to his hills,
His gun propped in the corner

Of the kitchen as he carried only
That swarm of squirming thoughts

So unsettled in his skull:
Why and where did his father go?

What should or could he do?
A college scholarship waited

In the fall for this oldest of
Ten, brothers and sisters galore.

They, too, waited and waited
Too his old mother growing old.

Too quickly growing old! So,
What could or should he do?

He left himself upon his ledge,
His red life coursing its rivered

Way overrunning the barrel, then
The stock where carefully carved

Before a friendly fire the night
After his first deer were the initials

A.K.

Around the Robin Egg, Aroo

Around the robin egg, Aroo,
A bent old man has naught to do
With birth. He's seen too much, It's fall.
Bent, caved in, and wheezing hard, all

His creaky parts protest and resent the toil
His paces put them through. Would oil
Help? Booze did not! That has been tried
For most the seventy years during which he died.

Ternion

I

Life is not an easy walk
Even if you drive through
In a Mercedes motor
Car and can toss a tip or two

For all the gods are not yet dead
Regardless of what is often said
They have their games within our groins
Their fancies are our agonies. Oh,

II

As our puny egos spurt and spin
Their balded tires in sandy lots of other men

Who receive so much more than we
Or so we think in enthusiastic jealousy

We burn our minutes up in haste
And stay together by twine and paste and waste. Oh,

III

Passes summer fall chill moon
Lay frosty pellets on petal and bloom
Tressy frozen down dead doom
Dressed in black in an empty room. Oh!

Bare Rump to Rump Old Lovers Lie

Bare rump to rump old lovers lie
Another night before they die.
They twitch and stir
And wheeze and snore,
It's not a pretty scene.
But their heart is in the right place:
Above the belly and below the face.

Bare rump to rump old lovers lie
And sounds of sleep exude;
But credit please where credit due
For they still sleep in the nude.

Bare rump to rump old lovers lie
In a sleep of mastered poses
As each turns to each, nose to nose,
And they entwine in a long embrace
While sleeping from heads to toes.

Bare rump to rump old lovers lie;
Their sleep it is so sound.
Alas! As if already in the ground.

I AM A RED SOX FAN

(Autumnal Ode)

I am a Red Sox fan!
I drive spikes through my hand,
I walk on beds of burning coals,
And sleep on a bed of nails.

I eat one bowl of rice each day,
Wear hair shirts,
Practice celibacy,
And stand naked in the cold, cold rain.

Oh, how I do love my pain.
I am a Red Sox fan!

OCTOBER RAINS

("Such was their burial of Hektor, breaker of horses."
– Homer)

I

The bay and chestnut mares stand still
   Among the brown and broken grass
Recently so green and rich upon the hill
   As now October days do pass

And leaves by biting rains are driven down,
   In all their furious colors spinning,
To the end of their days. Now the old town
   Attends the ends new beginning

As tall snows hover in the greying clouds
   And wait to speed the dying.
Soon it is done. But none of us admit aloud
   What we are or, that without trying,

We expect to live forever. Dumb, gentle horses stand;
   Big-headed dark-eyed gazing.
And I, scattered ash on the barren land,
   Have left but icy winds for grazing.

And this was the burial of Hektor, breaker
   Of horses? Not at all! Honored
Was he of men and gods. You can be sure that
   Only my dreams of death have you heard.

   II

   Hovering winds:
Go with me to endless days
   Or days end

   When my
Ghosted self outruns these
   Brittle bones

   And with its
Blathing lungs meekly blows
   Into your

   Long-winged
Arms. Around the town's
   Sad breast

   We'll go,
Collecting leaves and leaving
   Leaves to be

   Beaten by
October rains into the
   Hilly sod.

Proem and Poem

Proem

What we assume and see
May well not be.
For all that we can tell

We inch toward fire
In heaven or edge toward
Gods in hell.

Poem

Aesthetic eyes admire
The tasteful spires
Of New England
Churches couched in

Green of summer,
Green of spring,
Autumn gold or
Winter white.

I know
Just such a pair
Kept outside for
Four decades.

He left his pew
To others because
In poor Jesus
Lurks lurid Christophanies.

Believe what you will.
On our last day
We all lose.

Three Vagrants

(22/IX/63-Dallas)

Lulling on a knoll, three vagrants
    Slowly wine November
Noons away. Unlike busy ants
    By their boots they defer

To the drift of things, dust upon the
    Wind, until resound those
Shots and camera clicks which splayed
    Them into history.

Two Sonnets of a Sort as One Something

One

(He went into his hole)

He went into his hole
  Still waiting for life to be.
"What went wrong?" he asked
  The bearers of the pall.
Up the bleak wet wind walk to the knoll
Where Erma had ordered plots for two
In the old New England town
They climbed and considered.
She would follow soon,
Twelve years more, or ten,
Of bridge and TV
On a schedule firmly set

After World War II when it was confessed
That Henry had failed in faithfulness.

FALL

Two

(He had tried to get his life going, it was stalled)

He had tried to get his life going, it was stalled
But CPA's nailed to matriarchal architectural
Masterplans to scale the steep crevasse
Of those upping the wrungs into the upper
Middle class often die stillborn.
Meredith, daughter, only child, married
And much like her mother, never forgave
Till now when through a cornea streaked with tears she
Saw pebbles and dirt called "Dust" bounce off his box
With dull resound, drop, and settle upon the ground
As she, age eight in new birthday gown, jiggled
On his horsy-ride knee and swore she

Heard bearers of the pall choir their reply:
"Me? Me, too? O no God, no God, no, not me!"

DROMEDARY DOGMATIK

It will get more lonely still
As you slide your fingers to the gills

Of the Rainbow's head and find
All your efforts to be so kind

Are futile. The hook? Too deep!
The dangling guts, the steady seep

Of blood onto your cashmered wrist,
Pine coated hills hidden under mist,

And you stand solitary on the grey rock
Of your private estate where loons mock

FALL

You with protracted calls. Not one thing
Should you say in return. Sing

The appropriate monody, submit the
Entrails to the spiny lake, feed the

Ospreys of the air with
The bleeding, bulging-eyed myth

You clutch in hand, and do not attempt
To buy contrition or to repent

By trying to walk upon your water.

Is the Vermont Visitor Viennese?

    I

Piecemeal particles of prevention do
Endure, to be sure, but we must grasp
Quintessential things, a contour drawing,
A String Quartet, a monolog quite
Supreme

To redeem elemental prospects,
Abundant dreams of antiquated
Kings and Queens (and jacks and deuces)
Quite detrimental; hymns, laments,
Preludes,

All sorts of things: necklaces and rings
Buried beneath fallen leaves; buried
Under piles of leaves. Recite retained
Lines of poet song remembered in dreams.
Teacher,

Please, from Scarlet Taninger in trees,
Abandon not faith from those ancient dumb

Days. There is some good in good, of course!
Do you tune to forgotten chords of
Old ways?

II

Red leaves lolligag
Red leaves fall
Leaves brown and yellow
Dressing up the hall

Red leaves fluttering
Red leaves fall
Brown leaves blow away
Yellow leaves stay

   It's fall
   (Ist Wien)*

   It's fall
   (Ist Wien)

   It's fall
   (Ist Wien).

* *Ist Wien* is a phrase from the famous song 'Wien, du Stadt meiner Träume" (Vienna, City of My Dreams) by Rudolf Sieczynski which means "Is Vienna."

LATE FALL NIGHT BEFORE SLAUGHTER

Sprawling over the compass of
Our valley hills,

Its star-speckled blackness
Tightly tied to

Each corner of those old nobs,
A cold night,

Like some mythic monster, sends
Chills through our

Small, old barn shielding its keep
Where on golden
Grass of summer sleeps the
Penultimate

Sleep of pigs made fat to feed a
Winter hunger.

When Men Created Gods

When men created gods,
Long ago,
They did not know
All that we do today

About moons and sun,
The stars, the sea,
And how forms of life
Came to be.

But now that we know
A bit about who, what,
And why we are
It seems unfair,

If the diety
Is all powerful, good, and knowing,
Which is what the clergy
Does maintain,

It seems unfair
To retain something divine
Both to bless and to blame
By ascribing our unholy human mess
To some poor god's name.

ON THE MANNER BY WHICH MATTER
BECOMES SPIRIT

    I

On whiskey wings
We fly.
In whiskey arms
We die

A little, by and
by.
When whiskey sings
It brings

Earth, air, fire, sea
In me;
Mystic oneness
Sages

Would say: Pan of
All things
When whiskey sings.
Hoorah!

Hoorah! Hooray!
It sings
Then bears away
In sleep.

    II

Now whiskey lays
Me down
To sleep. I pray,
Maker,

My spirit keep
But should
I die before

I wake

I pray, Maker,
Take my
Spirit to blend
In that

Great oaken vat
To age
For years and years
Till when

My bottle's sold
For "Cheers."
Glasses rise, meet,
And clink

Then "Down the hatch"
Drinker
Goes now as drink
Since the

Maker's magic,
You see,
With my remains
Made yet

A different me
When from
My spirit wrought
Whiskey!

III

On whiskey wings
We fly.
In whiskey arms
We sleep.

In whiskey draughts
What once
We were we still
Do keep.

THRENODIES

    I
(Song of the aeons)

Hence five billion years one great orange
Orb expires cold and cosmic black.
What then will be our symphonies
Or middle age infidelities

Struck against boredom winding down
To death? Nothing then. Thus now our
Songs, our several loves, our small
Selves swelling with want and roaring need.

    II
(Flatbush lament)

To think upon all history dead,
Afloat in cold, dark void;
Our sun, charred ash, Shakespeare unsaid,
And Beethoven unhoid.

    III
(Old lovers air)

Old lovers, or lovers once, we
Should better say, for though they sleep
In one bed it is without any

Anticipation. They buss, then crawl
Through the day perfunctory.
No more passion do they see through

Thick spectacles. Old. We all come
To such an ignominious end
Upon a dull, flat road far from

Youthful expectations. Confess
What's so absurd; that the great highways of
Human life most of us will miss.

IV
(Duet of the dog and cat)

Each day we arise more near to
An end we somewhat fear.
End inexorable, we do
Not muse much on you yet hear

Stalking steps echo in our ears
At night in the long wait for
Sleep resisting. A dog barks, doors
Creak in late summer breezes,

Cats howl, while we, moons across
Grey faces, month by month, wait
For tomorrows to improve though
Knowing it's much too late.

V
(Dirge)

Today the secretary told
Of her friend's sister, not married
Very long, twenty-five years old,
Who after lunch, alone, carried

A shotgun to her car, then drove
Out an old dirt road, stopped, shot
Through the roof her troubled brain
And left remains in autumn rain.

VI
(Chorale)

Great death is no revelation.
Eating us all in the end we
Know that whether cancerous cells
Explode, hearts burst, or autos ram

Us down inevitably we
Die yet seldom know when death comes
And thus expound: live as if what
Life were left must be with us now.

My songs sing of death, of love:
Sing here of death more long than love.

Epilogue

(Testamentum)

Cremate, please!
Too much limb and pound
For little left
Precious ground.

Cremate, please!
Don't let those who care
Cage me, fancy-boxed,
Stuck there
Under ugly, marble-topped,
Phony-flowered mound.

Cremate, please!
Leave no hair on
Taxidermied skull
Nor jelly-stuffed flesh
On bony legs.

Cremate, please!
But save ashes few
For a minute glass
So my wife can
Time her eggs.

Peter Fox Smith lives in North Pomfret, Vermont over the mountains from where paternal ancestors made a home in St. Albans in 1763. His heritage is English, Scotch-Irish, and Swedish. Educated at University School, Denison University (B.A.), and Harvard University (M.A. and Ph.D.), he wrote his doctoral dissertation on Richard Wagner: *The Religious Dimension in Wagner's Art: A Study of his Parsifal*. Peter Fox Smith is a free-lance lecturer and a producer of over 1000 consecutive weekly classical radio programs for Vermont Public Radio. He plays wind and string instruments ("not in public"), even though when he was a boy his piano teacher successfully killed for almost a decade any capacity to play music. He began making poems in Middle School and that pleasure has survived the only course in poetry he ever took; a course in which he learned an invaluable lesson: do not risk a love for poetry by taking courses in poetry. Intensely individualistic, Peter is skeptical of almost any "school, cause, and creed." He loves reading, listening to music, making music, canoeing, ocean sailing, riding horseback, snowshoeing, and walking in the woods. Peter and his wife, Joanne, live on a small farm where they raised their two children, Peter and Alice, where they play with their grandchildren, Lauren and Andrew, and where they watch their gardens grow.